FLAMING ARROW ~ SERIES 3

© 2020 by Wong Lai Ching
Pen Name: Chingy

Published by
Wong Lai Ching
email: laiching10@yahoo.com

Edited by
Azmi Bin Anuar

For You To Behold ~

**Series 1 is a
Cleansing Foam**

**Series 2 makes
You Shine
& Bloom**

**Series 3 sets
You Free**

*Blood, Sweat & Tears are in it.

Nevertheless, Fresh Air & Sunshine

are present as well to meet the needs.

The Flaming Arrow ~ Series is written with the goal of drawing those who dislike poetry to gain a new appreciation for it. Creative writing of this nature is often disregarded, and I believe it's time for a comeback.

So much attention has been diverted to amassing wealth, running after motivation, and seeking inspiration. These are undeniably essential, but, how many of us give serious weight to Character-Building? Should we not be made aware of our ugly common traits that show up consistently?

In short, the Flaming Arrow ~ Series is designed for such a mission: clearing the foundations before receiving enhancement. It is an unobtrusive tool for awakening one's spirit to be made ready for healthy input that adds a sparkle in your soul.

CONTENTS

AMUSEMENT PARK

You've done nothing wrong ~ yet barred
from eating with the usual group;
leaving you all alone ~ feeling sad and
bad. But then, not too long after,
a pleasant surprise comes. It's the
Divine Merchant sending HIS Angel
to chauffeur you to dine with HIM
in HIS Banquet Hall. And, with that ~
you hop up onto the chariot with joy!

Note: Our Maker is watching over you.
HE will not leave you outside the door,
shivering in the cold.

~ Chingy

Flaws grow pale in the night
with every inch of anger
denied is Love found to abide
~ strong in its might.

Note: Where there is Love,
Forgiveness comes easy.

~ Chingy

Enjoy the piece of meat that is laid on your plate instead of nibbling on your neighbor's dish.

Note: Stop interfering with another's achievement while neglecting your own assignment.

~ Chingy

BATON PASSING

**When Trying stopped,
Victory ceased.**

**Note: Has Pride put you off
from Trying?**

~ Chingy

You multiply your Charm
without a kit when you
are Happy and Sweet.

Note: Inner beauty
emits a sweet spirit.

~ Chingy

BLEEDING ARTERY

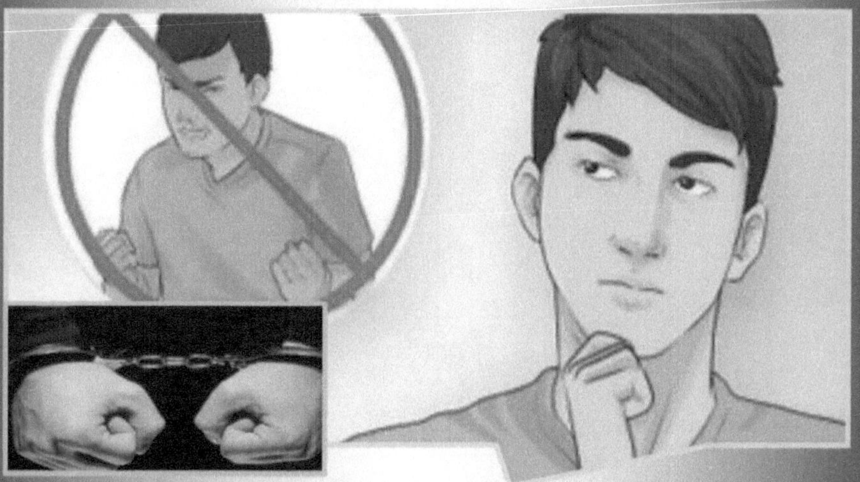

To dislike someone is nothing
more than self-torture.

~ Chingy

CHEWABLES

**Failure will soften our texture;
making us more approachable.**

~ Chingy

CONCRETE WALL

Never avoid settling issues of any
kind. With such, respect will
come your way duly unwind.

Note: When there are hesitations
and avoidance for clarification,
it hints of a guilty conscience.

~ Chingy

COOKING POT

Every one is created for a purpose.
Never deny your worth, or that you
can contribute to society with love.

Note: Being a true friend is an
invaluable contribution.

~ Chingy

Any refusal you face is another open attempt for exposure gain.

~ Chingy

Gaming with prejudice,
you gauge someone as shallow.
In the appearance of blind
hindsight ~ a humility
cry is at the door.

Note: The proud will be humbled.

~ Chingy

**Your mood is the role-play
of your health that forms the
paramount of your crown.**

**Note: Would you allow people
and circumstances to
control your emotions?**

~ Chingy

Walk straight and less
time will go to waste.

Note: Do the right thing (avoid white lies
and manipulation), and you will not
have to journey in unnecessary pain.

~ Chingy

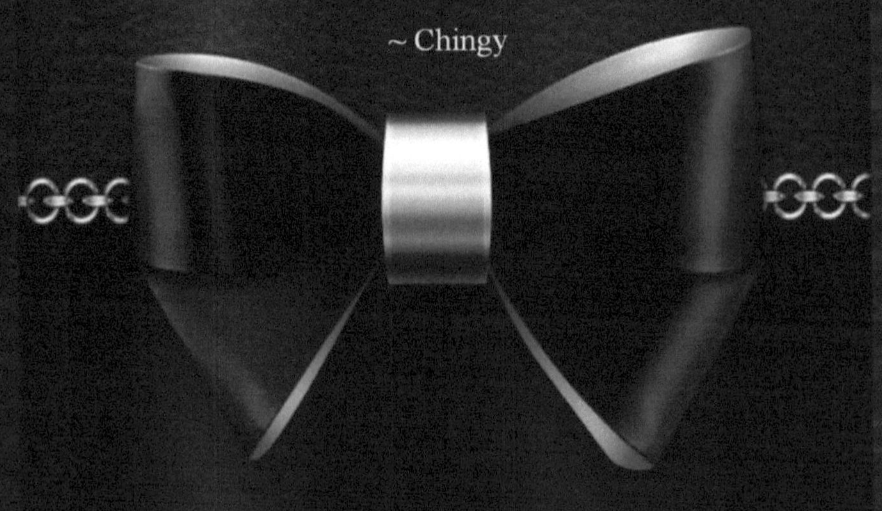

DUST FILTER

Disturbing noise will be on
the run when you are up
at the front.

Note: Allow not anyone to make fun
of you or your work to put you off
from becoming a forerunner.

~ Chingy

ENRICHED FARM

I don't know a lot, and it might be
a setback for me to reach the top.
But, I can always imitate GOD ~
that will help me hit the jackpot!

Note: Imitating GOD is
to follow in HIS footsteps.

~ Chingy

Don't get annoyed
with those trying
to outshine you ~
welcome what
they add on
to your notes.

Note: Those who are
trying to outshine you
are unconsciously
contributing
ideas to you.

~ Chingy

**Your tone of voice
is the commander
of the atmosphere.**

~ Chingy

**Less indulgence in your phone
to build a better home!**

**Note: Home implies "Accomplishments"
as well. Make your phone a slave
to you, not the other way round.**

~ Chingy

When
Love
is
not
at
the
entrance,
Murder
begins.

~ Chingy

FRUIT BASKET

**Put what you have into good use.
Food that is too sweet to eat on its
own need not be given away or
discarded. It can be used as a
sweetening substitute for our
dessert or breakfast cereal.**

**Note: Reputation can be saved
without reducing your stock.**

~ Chingy

Helping the weak is good.
Denying the strong is wrong.

Note: Denying can be in the form
of Indifference, that spells
subtle assassination.

~ Chingy

INVISIBLE CRIMINALS

You don't have to feel lousy
when good intentions shared
are not embraced.
The devil's hobby
is to attack you.

~ Chingy

MOVING TRAIN

When you can't get
what you want ~ be prepared
to receive a better next.

Note: Make the best
out of what you possess.

~ Chingy

**Misunderstandings always
arise when we choose
to bottle up
what we don't like.**

~ Chingy

**Stop fixing what you can't
and start knitting your gown.**

~ Chingy

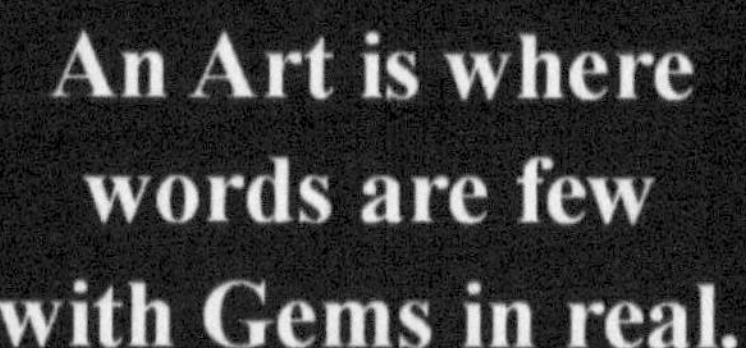

An Art is where
words are few
with Gems in real.

Note: Less words ~ more
attention gained.

~ Chingy

You have the Power to make
someone Glad or Sad every day.

Note: Nothing extended or withheld
will appear small in the eyes of
the receiver, as it will be well
recorded in the heart ~ either
with gratitude or dismay.

~ Chingy

PARTY NIGHT

May I steal your time a little to
have a sweet moment together?

Note: Having self-control is needful.
Acting on how you feel
is pampering your desire
that can lead you into trouble.

~ Chingy

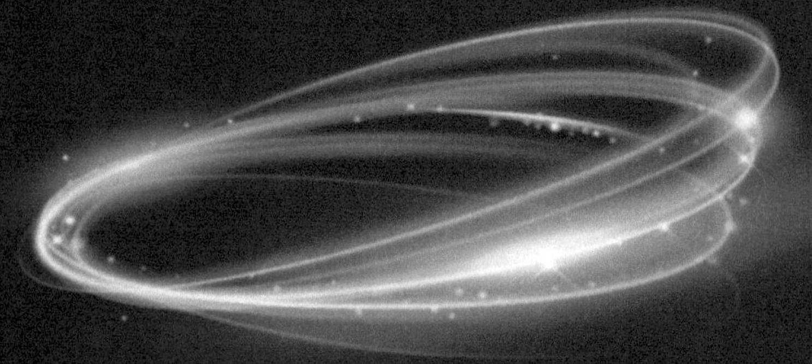

**Show me how to spin
if you want me to win.**

~ Chingy

**A soft look with a strong mind
is the combination of an
expensive wine.**

**Note: Soft look - kind face;
Strong mind - trustworthy and
steady (not easily influenced).**

~ Chingy

Your Pride.

One's Life.

Which

would

you place

at the

Front

Line?

~ Chingy

**A Blessing Angel might use
your enemy's constructive voice
to deliver your joyful song.**

**Note: It's difficult to sit at your
enemy's feet. But would you ~
if you get to benefit from it?**

~ Chingy

You can't type
without knowing
how to write.

Note: Don't waste time
on what you're
not gifted in.

~ Chingy

**To admit you are "No Angel"
while neglecting a
"Self-edit" will stagnate
you in a depriving swamp.**

~ Chingy

**For each loving deed we sow,
a fruitful plant will grow.**

~ Chingy

With Improvement sitting next
to Correction, a fine duet
is in play for you.

Note: We should listen to correction
without a selective attitude.
Those who want you
to improve will correct you.
There is no reason to disrupt peace
and risk their favor from you.

~ Chingy

SKYLINE GLOW

**Every one is filled with a flame
to reign within their claim.**

**Note: Discover your talent and
excel in it. Encouraging others
is an honorable gift.**

~ Chingy

Forgive those who refuse to support you as they might not have enough courage to do so.

Note: Be it in any aspect.

~ Chingy

You set fire to your name
and poverty to your claim
for the negative you choose.

Note: Anything unloving is negative,
including unconscious time abuse.

~ Chingy

A duplicate can never overrule
the original that dominates
the pinnacle of attention.

Note: Beware of imitators
stealing banners to claim
as their own.

~ Chingy

**Self-encouragement is Crucial,
as you might not receive enough
wind to set your boat on sail.**

**Note: Not many will have
time to cheer for you.**

~ Chingy

Let opinions
come but no one
should dominate
the final say,
except you.

Note: Do not allow
others to decide
for you nor decide
for others, unless
it is necessary.

~ Chingy

**Rich or Poor
~ Daddy
got to dip
into his
pocket
to
Provide
for a
Family
that
Honors
him as
the Head
with Pride.**

~ Chingy

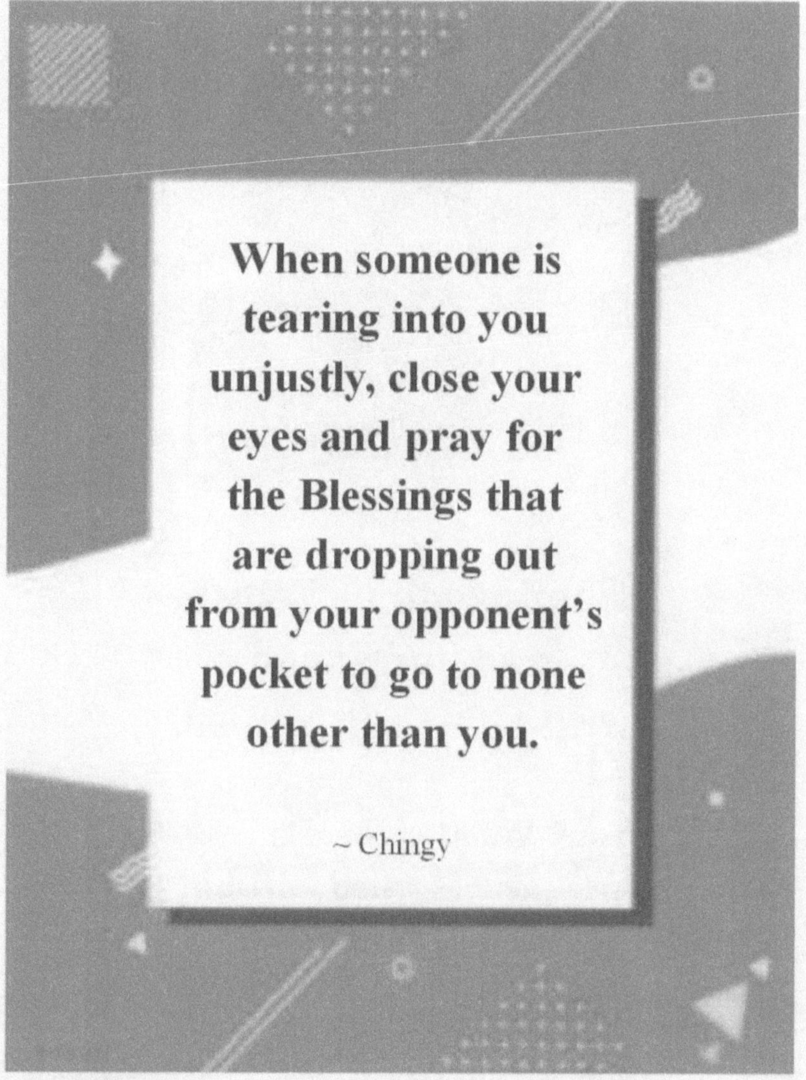
When someone is
tearing into you
unjustly, close your
eyes and pray for
the Blessings that
are dropping out
from your opponent's
pocket to go to none
other than you.

~ Chingy

**Continue to be Selfish,
and our Favor
with GOD will Vanish.**

**Note: We often overlook the
consequences when selfishness
is embedded in us.**

~ Chingy

**The Love
of a Mom
is an
Immeasurable
Run.**

~ Chingy

**Being Racist is similar
to that of a Terrorist.**

**Note: We cannot hold on to
untaught principles to ward off
coronavirus and any other
infliction to come.**

~ Chingy

WATERPROOF

Vengeance
is a sweet,
tempting
rose.
To the one
who can
withhold ~
will stand
strong
as a
winsome
pole.

~ Chingy

A
clever
mind
is
never
proud
or
unkind.

~ Chingy

WRONG CALCULATION

Taking advantage
of others
will lead
you to a
disadvantageous
end.
If you don't
believe it,
you may
proceed.

~ Chingy

CONCLUDING NOTES

Another hurdle cleared! I would not have been able to accomplish it without the help of the Almighty, truly! Much of this has been written and compiled over the years ~ and what more can I add on? But not when GOD is involved.

Prophecies were given to me one after another without me seeking for them ~ they sustained me and kept me going. I cannot find words enough to express GOD's goodness. In short, HE is so sweet and smart! I pray that the Sovereign Lord will anoint me continually as I avail myself to be used for HIS Glory.

Herein, I would like to thank all who graciously and consistently prayed for me, extended valuable opinions without reservation, and sponsored / purchased the Flaming Arrow ~ Series, serving as my needed pillars. May GOD Bless you all for the kindness you have shown me. Sincerely, I remain.